Oh Boy Summer!

Diahann Darwood

Illustrated By Niaren Binford

For Noah and Autumn, who love nature

For Derrell, who inspires

And for Max, who encourages

I love you all

Creation Stirred Inc.
15 Landau Lane
New Hempstead, NY 10977
www.CreationStirred.com

Printed in the United States of America

First Printing, 2013

Be like the flower,
turn your face to the sun.

-- Kahlil Gibran

Lebanese American artist, poet, and writer; the third best-selling poet of all time 1883 to 1931

Summer sneaks in and

playfully comes around,

One minute it's raining,

then there's sun

beating on the ground.

What if the sun

never went down?

Summer is happy to smother us
with his heat,
Making us sweat as we walk
playfully down the street.
What if we walked down the road
with bare feet?

Summer invites us to splash
at a pool or on the beach.

That's why he puts the cool days

just beyond our reach!

What if it were summer all year,

when would teachers teach?

But we love you Summer,

because it's our time to be free!

Summer says, "Wear your

sunglasses, your sandals,

and throw on your best tees!"

What if Summer is a kid,

just like you and me?

When Summer is here,

everyone comes out to play.

Adults are cooking outside

on the hottest days!

What if Summer whispered,

'play play, play'?

Summer yells, "Block parties,

picnics, pool diving everywhere!

I'll beat you in a street-race

if you dare!"

In the summer time,

I wonder if the kids all over the

world run around without a care!

School? Homework?

Yellow school bus?

No.

It's swimming or baseball where

the coaches cheer and fuss!

What if there was a swimming pool

and baseball field

in the backyard for us?

Summer says, "Travel the world, go camping, vacate! Next year we start all over, and I can't wait!"

I wonder if Summer wakes up early and stays up late?

Summer Science is Everywhere!

Find out more…

Why does the sun feel warmer

in the summer than winter?

How do different animals

stay cool in the summer heat?

Which animals live in warm waters?

Cold waters?

What can sand be used to make?

Can you…

Create a diorama or illustration of

an animal in a very hot environment?

Find out how long it takes ice to melt outside

on a summer morning? A summer afternoon?

A summer evening?

Track the weather for 7 days (or more)?

Temperature? Sun? Clouds? Rain?

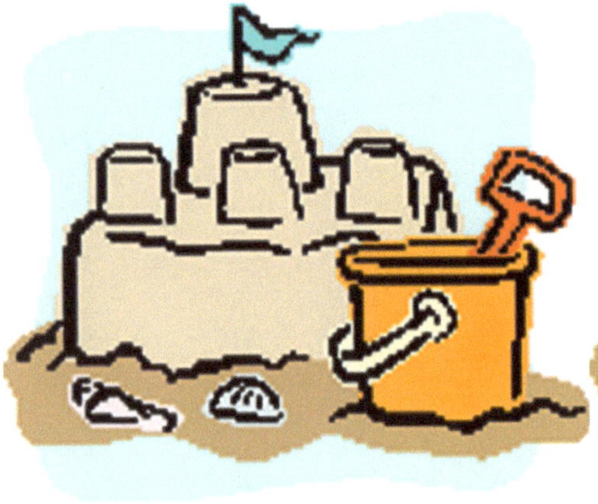
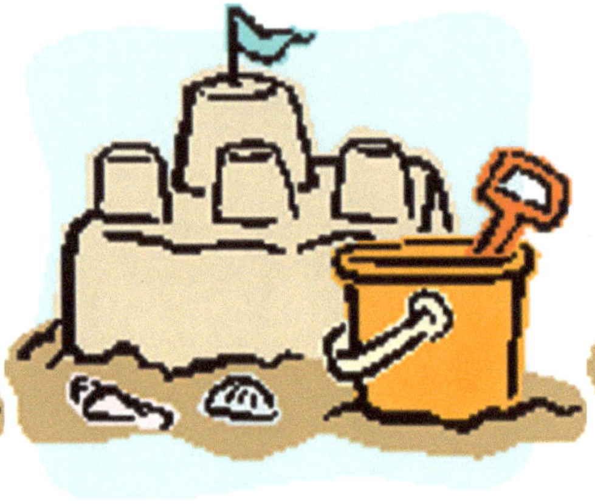
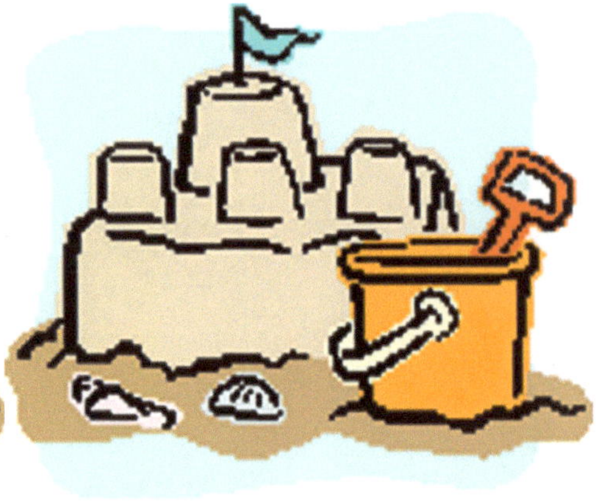
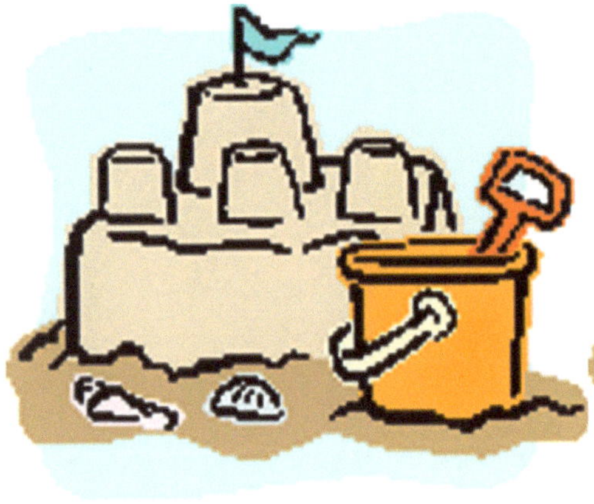
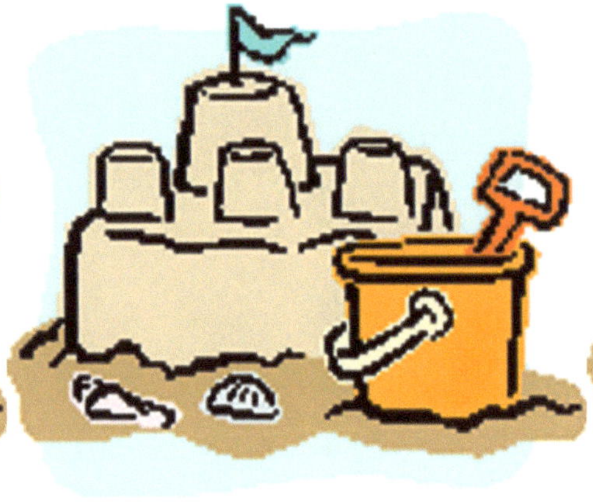
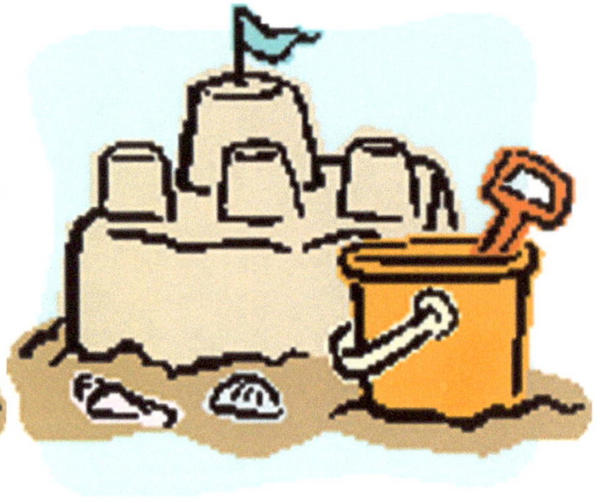
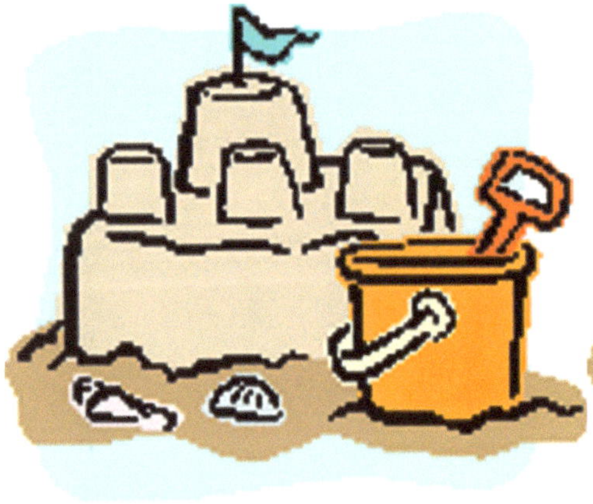
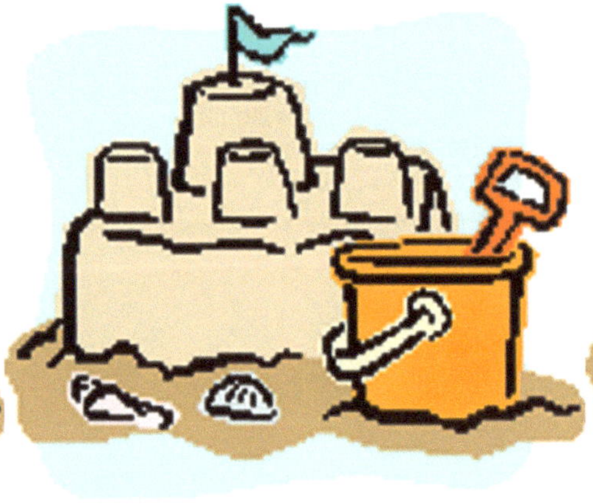
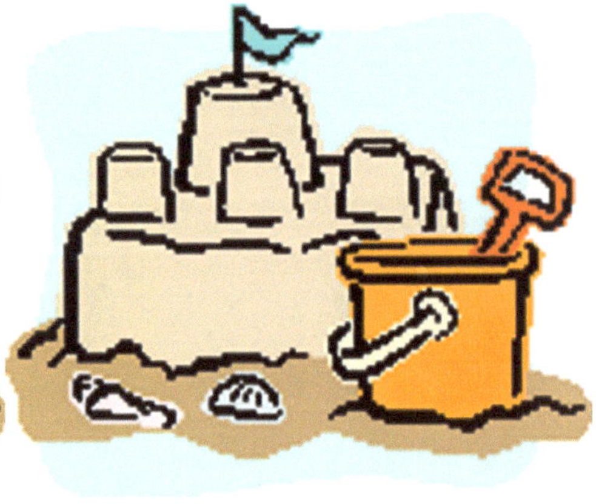